THE LIFELINE TREMBLES

Poems by
Mary Kay Rummel

BLUE LIGHT PRESS ◆ 1ST WORLD PUBLISHING

1ˢᵗ WORLD
PUBLISHING

SAN FRANCISCO ◆ FAIRFIELD ◆ DELHI

THE LIFELINE TREMBLES
WINNER OF THE 2014 BLUE LIGHT BOOK AWARD
Copyright ©2014 by Mary Kay Rummel

1ST WORLD LIBRARY
PO Box 2211
Fairfield, Iowa 52556
www.1stworldpublishing.com

BLUE LIGHT PRESS
www.bluelightpress.com
Email: bluelightpress@aol.com

BOOK, COVER DESIGN
AND INTERIOR DRAWINGS
Melanie Gendron

COVER PHOTOGRAPH
It Is The Same Story
by Hervé Constant

AUTHOR PHOTO
Gary Silva, Silva and Silva Photography

FIRST EDITION

LCCN: 2014940886

ISBN 978-1-59540-929-4

THANK YOU TO THOSE WHO HELPED MAKE THIS BOOK POSSIBLE:

London artist Hervé Constant for the cover photograph, *It Is The Same Story*, and other poetry-inspiring work;

Sandra Rummel for her help with cover design and Melanie Gendron, designer for Blue Light Press Books;

My husband, Conrad, for his continuing strong support;

Maia who has read so many of these poems in various stages and whose insight into poetry is continually amazing;

Diane Frank, Editor in Chief of Blue Light Press who inspired and helped shape the poems. This book would not exist without her generosity and insight;

members of the Blue Light Press online workshop group who read much of this work in early stages;

members of the Onionskin writing group, Sharon Chmielarz, Kate Dayton, Carol Masters, Nancy Raeburn, Martha Meek and Cary Waterman, especially Patricia Barone for her close reading of the manuscript and Margaret Hasse for the title idea;

the Ventura County Arts Council who appointed me Poet Laureate of Ventura County;

Jim Rogers and Eamonn Wall for their blurbs;

Jackson Wheeler, Kevin and Patti Sullivan, Phil Taggart, Marsha de la O,

the Ventura Thursday night poets and all the hosts who have invited me to read;

Elizabeth Quintero and all the people who come to readings and buy books.

Thanks always to Tim, Miranda and Sylvie, Ann, Andrew, Mari and Libby for their inspiration.

ACKNOWLEDGEMENTS

Thank you to the editors who selected these poems for publication.

Literary Journals
Artlife (on permanent display at the Los Angeles County Museum of Art) ~ "Days We Wear Like Earrings"
Askew ~ "Palimpsest"
Cartier Street Review ~ "Dreaming in Orange"
Ekphrasis ~ "A Beltane Tapestry"
Fiction Week Literary Review ~ "Beached Whale at Point Mugu"
Journal of Language and Literacy Education (Fall, 2013) ~ "Ars Poetica"
Loonfeather ~ "Sexual Territories"
Nimrod ~ "If Not Snow," "Burnt Dress," "Lost: A Sister's Tale"
Pirene's Fountain ~ "Wounded Angel," "For Us Who Are Afraid," "The Road," "Reading Zagajewski in Prague"
St. Paul Almanac ~ "Coming Home," "River Cop," "Why I Love to Write"
Ventana Monthly ~ "Ars Poetica"
Whistling Shade ~ "Lost, A Sisters Story," "River Cop"

Anthologies
And the Humming: Poems About Grandparents ~ "Ars Poetica"
Daring to Repair (Wising Up Press) ~ "Painting the Walls," "Sometimes An Angel"
Corners of the Mouth: A Celebration of Thirty Years at the Annual San Luis Obispo Poetry Festival ~ "Field Walking in County Donegal"
First Water: Best of Pirene's Fountain (Glass Lyre Press) ~ "Wounded Angel"
Meditations on Divine Names (Moonrise Press) ~ "The Poet Goes Fishing"

River of Earth and Sky: Poems for the 21st Century (Blue Light Press) ~ "The Dream Theater," "Poppies in the Ruins," "One Hundred Sand and Flower Carpets"
Storytelling: A Path to our Future. Rummel & Quintero. Peter Lang Publishing ~ "Between Rivers"
The Heart of All That Is: Reflections on Home (Holy Cow! Press) ~ "Between Times"

Woman in Metaphor, an artist's book by Stephen Linsteadt ~ "Wounded Angel"
"Solstice Suite: A poem sequence" was performed with pianist Gwen Perun.

Several of these poems appeared in first versions on northography. com and were inspired by photographs of art works posted there by Britt Fleming.

Prizes
Irish American Crossroads Prize ~ "Ars Poetica," "What Stone Knows"
Ventura Country Writers Prize ~ "Sometimes an Angel"
Pushcart Nominations ~ "A Beltane Tapestry," "The Poet Goes Fishing"

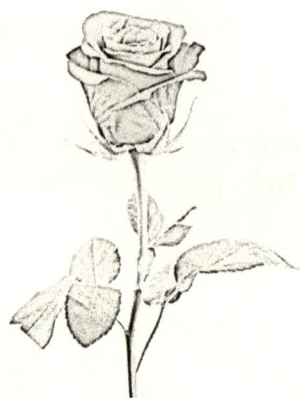

For Sylvie Jane

From what I have heard of love,
people don't give their heart.
Our heart flies from us,
and we can choose to follow or not.

Brian Friel — Translations

Table of Contents

I

The Weave in the Cloth of the World

II

Solstice Suite: A Poem Sequence

III

Sometimes An Angel

IV

Poppies in the Ruins

1

The Weave in the Cloth of the World

*...I had to see
and not just know, to see clearly
the sights and fires of a single world...*

Adam Zagajewski ~To See

Tapestries: A Poem Sequence

A Beltane Tapestry

Wings flicker as they dip to yarrow,
monkshood, brambles, meadowsweet,
doves hidden in leaves.

Move back a step and you'll see
a gold thread running through,
one harp chord, the demanding,
voice of desire.

Your eye forgets the dancing,
the birds, the piper,
the millefleured world
where a tower floats on a hill,
turrets lost in threadbare clouds.

Shine is all you see.
It glitters, seduces
in this ordered fading world.

Suddenly you tremble,
a lone poplar welcoming
its finches home.

The Unicorn Tapestries

1

I Have Come Back to You, City of Light

Only your colors can save me now.

No longer the mother
of two young boys who ran
from sword to arrow in war museums.

No longer the poet who wrote
too much of Manet's dark canvas—
the young man going off to war,
the wells of his mother's eyes.

No longer the woman wandering
crypts beneath gothic cathedrals.

I still love narrow streets, illusions—
city of shadows, paint me with stone.

At Cluny the white haired lady
holds her jewels to the light
then gives them to the unicorn.
A mon seul desir.

I am a blue arabesque.
guided by an amethyst star.

Red tipped palette of the past,
let me live in love again,
*let my heart be feral
to my own desire.*

Only your light can save me now.

2

To My One Desire

It's time to give you away now
my chest full of words,
tongue-flood, my one desire—
lark, scent of cardamom,
lilac moon.

Words are the colors I swim.
My heart the cartographer
charts the water, sweeps
back as the tide turns,
as pale world gathers its skin
into pearl, onyx, coral.

I've forgotten more times
than gulls cross the morning
how to let go.

The Bayeaux Tapestry

1

Le Chevalier

He aches for silence
with nothing to forgive.
No birds except hawks
keeping their brown watch.

His morning standard was clear:
chains of metal,
red lions crouching on shields,
white banners fluttering on a breeze.

Not defeat, not abandoning the dead.
Since there was no escape
he feinted and dodged,
but cunning failed like an old tale.

He fell towards sleep hoping for death.
Blank eyes opened inside his night.
Irony grew, choked all belief.

A few patient horses and dogs returned.
How surprised he was to find them whole,
settled with rabbits and field mice
into what had been his soul.

2

The Conscript

He didn't know he would be grateful
for a late autumn journey
where every step splintered time.

He didn't know he would enter
music that translates the world
back into umber fields
that named him stone,
hut, cluster of lavender

as if he were a root come
out of the earth
or a lost boy fed by hungry
ghosts or angels.

Gardens of Paris

1

At the Rue de Varenne, Rodin's Thinker
rules the rose garden,
his bronze thoughts lost to you and me.
He appears again, brooding above
the last judgment doors.

Carved beneath him, eternity's lovers
twist in the embrace of the damned,
to yearn but never touch,
lovers who grasp for each other
as demons drag them to the fire.

A blackbird sings his searching song.
We walk beneath linden trees
in our aging bodies where desire
simmers after all these years.

Chimney swifts shrill in chorus
diving for midges in the long dusk.
Peonies droop in every triangle of garden
as we cross the plaza behind Notre Dame,
the bridge over the Seine crowded
with spirits—the living licking ice cream
and the dead still hungry.

2

Tonight the sound-garden
of a Bach concerto drifts from
a medieval church off the Rue St. Jacques.

Silence rises from the Roman dig
at Musée de Cluny
from rooms of marble statues
saints and kings without arms.
The two of us quiet now as the patisserie
at the end of a long day.

We praise the garden of the courtly lover
and the monks' medieval herbs
fresh as oranges luminous in market stalls.

Praise the short stairway
as we climb to our room.
Praise my heart, still strong.
Praise your body, still whole—
our night's story not yet over.

A rectangle of light spills
through the high window.
I paint you Notre Dame blue.
I am Sainte-Chapelle red. Together,
we're purple in the deep
Paris night.

The Time of Peonies

for Tim

I want to come back each May in opulent blossoms,
in a full bellied amplitude of flesh.
A Renoir bather with sunlight stippling
luminous breasts—rosy nipples
a ripe brown berry centering the swell.

The profligate peonies splurge it all,
even as petals fall eroded and whispering
cream and raspberry to the earth.

For you and me no more dancing.
We breathe the end of the tango.
Our bodies carry on past their own borders.

All his life Renoir caressed
the limpidity of flesh, and even now
we breathe the quickened breath of appetite.

Today let's rub pearls of peony blossoms
over chests, bellies, legs,
backsides dappled by sun,
following the light that slides from nipple
down to shadowy thigh.

Heat on bare heads, steaming shoulders,
we smile in our paeonic bodies.

One Hundred Sand and Flower Carpets: Guatemala

I'm kind of like a priest of the religion of art and beauty.
~Bill Teeple, Painter

They began last night and are working still
at noon, even the little ones who spray
dyed vermillion and orange sand grains
to keep them from blowing away.
Their mother in jeans and sweatshirt stretches
to set the topaz eyes in the Quetzal birds
and the shadows on Mary's roses.

Mary with long hair, real as theirs or mine,
aquamarine stones for her eyes, holds the child
at the center of the universe, butterflies gracing
each pole. The young woman with earphones
and her cousin with a cell phone, lay down
serpentine borders of purple hibiscus.

They keep me awake all night but the beauty
at my feet pushes faithlessness away.
Soon clouds of incense dark the narrow street.
Bare feet of men bearing a statue of Jesus
destroy the carpet while drums mourn
and the children sweep up brilliant fragments. . .

What happens to beauty when no one believes anymore?

Ars Poetica

After Jackson Wheeler

Because my mother's mother carried her Irish language
across a stormy Atlantic to St. Paul

Because my great grandfather who lived to be 100
sang in Irish as he bounced us on his bony leg

Because on the front porch of my grandmother's house
the cousins, all named Mary,
learned 100 names for green from rebel songs

Because I lived sixty years before I learned my mother's father
died drunk under the hooves of a horse he was driving

Because my cousin, Sheriff O'Connell, who took bribes from
Chicago gangsters, gave money to my widowed grandmother

Because when I read about him in St. Paul histories
I thought saint not sinner

Because my father's tiny mother came from Galway
with a family too full of priests and nuns

Because she loved to talk in the way of Irish women
over tea and toast at small tables

Because I grew up in the quotidian music of women's murmuring
close to the ground where the world begins

Because men were either silent or overbearing
I lived my girl's life with *Ann of Green Gables* and *Little Women*

the bus plying the Old Fort Road to school
became my *Bridge at San Luis Rey*

Because art and music were in the church
I thought beauty belonged to God

Because roots of my young astonishment
cling to my inner life like the pine cone—growing
even after fire, living scales

Because in the convent we were told to be silent
I picked up a pen

Because of my heart's homelessness

Because a poem waits for me to see it
the way Monet's last painting
his exact pink and red primroses
waited for his uncurtained vision

Because love will not let go

Because words un-write as they are written
un-speak as they are spoken

Because my granddaughters
listen to my tales of trolls and beanstalks
their eyes pools where words sink and grow
the way I once listened to the old ones

 I do not want to die without writing
my watery unwritten universe.

What Stone Knows

Dingle, Ireland

These naked fields where one's voice must go
into an orphaned silence, where blackbirds
whistle a challenge to fishing boats,
where night wanderers, moon loving creatures
seek a crevice of shade.

Autumn air tintinnabulates, as sunlight
caresses the slant of carved symbols
in the Ogham stone.

I trace their lines, hungry for names
as if they were not already deep in me,
words saying what stone knows.

My hands begin to speak at sunrise,
say my hungry heart is a blackbird.
Earth keeps my feet fastened to flesh
but my body like a heliotrope turns
toward bright red needles, liquid fire,
the composition of light.

From stone walls called *lace*, blackbirds sing.
The soul is granite cliffs, open sea, island.
We must find our way there.

Sexual Territories—1988

Sandymount Strand, Dublin

Beside James Joyce's tower, I sit
on forbidden rocks, every day ignoring
the *men only* sign
marking the place where they swim nude.

Inside the round tower, a museum
for the almost blind master's manuscripts,
magnifying glass and black eye patch.

Today a woman jumped in naked.
TV crews caught her springing flesh
white where the sun never touched her.

Two hundred people came to gawk.
Underneath the waves, divers with cameras.

Seeing through his blindness, Joyce found
inside himself Leopold and Molly and the words
to tell how we are men and women both.

Now the ocean batters rock
while the poet's dark eye patch circles
like a raven over the disbelieving crowd
crying *see. . . see. . .*

For Us Who Are Afraid

La Antigua, Guatemala

Sometimes the air is fresh with the smell of lemons
but not today when clouds parade around volcanoes,
mountains hide from mountains.
Today the air purples with incense billowing
from censors swung by small boys.

Funeral marches roll over the city from brass horns,
slow beat, slow step of drums, slow desolation rising.
Forty children carry Jesus and his mother
through the narrow streets.

The barge with Jesus goes by. His mother's stops.
I look into her painted eyes, wishing she could see
beyond these girls in white who carry her. Could see
children dying in Guatemala, Mexico, North American pueblos.

If she could see beyond these boys dressed like Roman soldiers
to children dying in Darfur, Somalia, Palestine,
in Rwanda, Bosnia, Afghanistan, Iraq, Syria.
The names of the dying—the weave in the cloth of this world.

When she first saw her son she rejoiced in toes
small as kernels of corn, ears covered with down.
She was the lemon tree, and he, the tiny hungry finch.

Did she know men prayed as they began to kill each other?
Soldiers still caught inside the war drums,
and the procession marches on.

Reading Zagajewski in Prague

At a black marble table in the Cafe Louvre
your poems pull me deep into hallways
worn with age and graffiti where the city
wears black undergarments and eternity
dresses in ruins.

Poland is your home, near enough
to feel your spirit in these cobbled streets
still peopled by men in black wool,
caps pulled low on their foreheads.

I could find you on the corner where a string quartet
plays Mozart, melodies threading the screams
of generations, in the bass and treble clef
of *Dvorak's Cello Concerto*, or at the Jewish memorial—
names carved into the wall, names like bird song
in the saddest neighborhoods.

Your poems flicker in eyes of gargoyles,
wander among rooftop saints
where classical and rococo hold hands.

I could find you in the square where parents, professors,
clear-throated flutists and poets await your greeting,
the dead and the living threading plazas,
church yards, like deep fish through dark rivers.

Soon I'll sit on a bench facing the sea.
While Prague's blooming trees still quiver,
I'll remember the gold and cream of the city
and your words, moving in its shadows,
branches of kelp inside the waves' green swell.

The Vastness Around Her

(House of Mary—Ephesus, Turkey)

When I was young I knelt before her
squinting my eyes, willing the stone
to smile, alabaster face at the side altar
too sweet, unlike this carved face before me,
now like Artemis, mother goddess.

Mary lived on this mountain above orchards,
vineyards spreading to the Aegean.
I kneel on a patterned carpet, lay my fears
before her, light candles for my loves—
the litany of names explodes.

In the Muslim town below, women and old men
still snap beans outside blue doors
beneath vine leaves and flower boxes.
Up the next mountain in an old Greek village
tourists sip fruit wine, buy small tiles—
blossoms with turquoise leaves, plum-red centers.

Mother, at the time when the little cicada
would have been praying, I sing
to you, rocking like the sea
at the edge of my abyss.

Beautiful One, this is how
you crooned inside me when I was
too young to know anything
of doubt.

I will stay here, almost able to live
on color alone, leaves and stems, sweet pea,
morning glory tendrils—words I've stored
spill out, stories that begin in whispered litanies
and end with mountain jays.

Istanbul Winged

Indigo islands raise up a city of merchants
stringing bridges, erecting a palace
hermetic as a jewel box.

The sky spreads, indifferent,
across layered history, unloading
sparse cargo of summer clouds.

By late afternoon, the last boat
to the Black Sea slips
gracefully out of the harbor

where small dolphins leap
between ferries and black tankers—
liquid turquoise.

Tonight seventy ships line up
begging berth in Istanbul port.

A shuffling man brings roasted lamb wrapped
in newsprint through the darkening alley—

sky brewed to the hue of smoked tea
haunted by flame,
stars like sparks in a somnolent brazier.

Prayers, call and response from giant mosques
echo among ancient, humble buildings.
A holy tree here, a goddess I once knelt to.

Painted-over mosaics and frescoes
bleed like silver moonlight
through thin white clouds.

Blind, Winged, Dazzled

Forget snow, frost's repeated pinch,
sadness of mall-glitter, empty streets,
the drag of thwarted Sundays.

On the California coast
you are fed by the orange-gold
aureole, nipple of the sun-breast
our mother who art. . .

warm fruit-breath of hibiscus
savor of cherries on the tongue
sunlight bees on water.

On the sea-arched horizon
a single tall ship carries
a light-pyramid, the violet eye,
receiver of color for winds
spirit-laced, mast-bells turning
in heaven and on earth. . .

You will hear hidden thoughts of strangers,
longtime lovers holding hands on the beach
who can't stop staring at islands snared
in violet, azure netted with primrose
all hallowed. . .

Forget everything
and maybe you will see
her kingdom coming. . .

the way sometimes on the boardwalk,
the sun struck eyes of a beggar
look into yours and suddenly
you evaporate.

Beached Whale at Point Mugu

They say the whale slammed into a ship.
Her great grey corpse floated east
twenty-six miles, carried by Channel tides
and currents to this shingled beach.

In our minds the whale still heaves
against splatter and squall, erupting,
falling back, power translating
to bone and fat and muscle
until the driving spirit leaves.

We can't turn away, but breach ourselves,
heaving sideways out of old visions,
seeing with ears and noses.
In the silence below all things,
those few moments of sunrise—
anemone opening deep purple
melody of oil-shining streets—
we believe in muscle, hidden bone
and soft, soft flesh.

Every scrap of clothing worn near the body
has to be burned. Even our shoes reek
of oily decay spilling into sand.
Only the whale shaped trench remains
to be bitten away by the sea
that would have taken all.

And we are left, lashed to hands and faces,
breath cascading throat to lungs,
simple and tortuous as the journey
of water over rock now rising
in the spray, shivering,
plunging into silence, drifting
seaward, always wanting
like water, to be somewhere else.

Ordinary Time

I learned time on my knees
measured by red rosary beads,
sorrowful mysteries always
followed by joyful, distant glorious.

I was learning what to keep
and what to toss away.
Recursive recumbent lesson—
I make a myth of it,
but it was ordinary.

Common as my feet sinking
into sand, toes gripping
as I walk along the freshwater
invisible in the miracle of light.

My spirit tries to remember
how the mind can reinvent beauty,
a tawny throated wind
in the sea song of timothy grass.

A mother and nine baby ducks
celebrate another night of outwitting
the cats, raccoons, and fox.

Every day I see the single
unforgettable thing
shining against the large,
hummingbird aerialist,
an eagle skimming the pines,
a turtle rising from the mud,
bedazzling

everyday mysteries made of the holy
shaking out of murky depths—
a Brahms sextet or the sun burnt woman
sleeping on the beach
next to what she owns.

Shifting Time

After Adam Zagajewski

Music we hear together
stays with us always.

Mahler's adagietto, a cerulean door in a wall
and behind the door, lenticular clouds
the melody, both door and weightless key.

Mendelssohn's heart breaking chords,
Beethoven in the art deco palace.
Melodies we could see.

Dvorak's Seventh in Prague's Smetana Hall
a wedding cake, all gold and cream.
Music we tasted.

In the car Bach shimmers
the air between us.

Gregorian chants ring inside us.
When we were young,
the monks' stained glass voices
became our own.

Music we hear together
lives in us always.

Koko Taylor pierced us with blues
beside Lake Superior in the rain, with steel
blazing on Chicago's wind blown streets.

We knelt in a mud soaked tent,
transfixed by Coltrane's "Love Supreme."

At U2's Rose Bowl liturgy, we danced
in exuberance to songs of the forgotten,
the wronged, the mute, the absent, the dead.
Gave voice to those who were quiet in life.

We heard strings above the city
plunged in darkness,
breathing slowly over a scorched earth,
a gliding lament lifting
the lilac's black leaves.

Brahm's Violin Concerto
a message from beyond time
tells us the world at its edges
changes to love and is fragile.

The cello's almost human voice,
a sunburst of wings
on the lowest strings,
will be what's left of speech
between us.

Praise from the Edges

Walking pathless woods, I praise
overgrown thistles and hawthorn.
A little horse that comes from a new forest
teaches me to sing what is misplaced
on the knife edge of the world.

Even in broken glass
I find a shape-changer's magic—
crows feeding on tossed out bones, fish
nosing the bottom of sewage pools, the fox
lurking in a landscape of blown cartons.

I stumble through underbrush avoiding snakes,
shaking off flies and mosquitoes.
Water glitters in the abandoned courtyard pool
outside the old abbey where I hear
the scree-slide of crickets in oat grass.

Chants no longer rise and fall behind the cloister,
but the hands of angels are a choir
where ancestors hide in other lives
murmuring half-taught names in the dark.

Time to catch the descending feast
of silence in the feathers of water birds,
a staggered arising
from dark sleeves of the marsh,
a whisper at the edge of the mind.

Moonlight opens a ragged white flower.
Blackbird sings its three notes twice.
So much blue humming
across darkening airways,
white feathers—skylights of the world.

Hours of looking pass before I hear
waves of elephant songs,
wind, rain stick, sift of water

through rock, and underneath it all
an almost human singing.

Analemma

The position of the sun plotted every day for a year
at the same time, in the same place,
creates the shape of a figure 8.

A lost girl once circled
the ghosted center of the Cathedral
and imagined lightning splitting the roof
above the ruby light on the altar,
the eye that never closed.
Who are you? A life of asking.

Sometimes she wandered
the tangled banks of the Mississippi,
in her ears wind whine, on her skin nail rain.

A blue heron balanced at the core of things,
pulsing in the green until it rose
on chalybeous wings, easily shifting air.
The girl loved that lifting from earth to sky
the breathy puff of wings.

She felt them passing through her—
moths, grasshoppers, monarchs,
hummingbirds, bees,
drumming long-silenced,
a meandering river of oscillating wings
arriving, blessing, departing—
as if she were the center of a figure eight
with everything flowing home to the sun.

Raiment

A cloak of light thrown over our heads
blinds us to crescents of Venus,
glitter of riverine crystal, crimson aurora,
great spilling Milky Way.

In an eccentric sea of stars
we make up our bed—
heads at the North Star,
feet toward Sagittarius,
limbs flung to the cardinal points,
unpredictable as our hearts.

We'll sleep under a tapestry of rain
while a magician's cloak
of emerald, saffron, sapphire
threads through our lives, our nights
bound by ripe persimmon,
cavernous rose.

We wake still earth bound
to a world of dun and leached green,
Spanish moss, hedge apple.
We wake remembering colors, grateful
that filipendulous monarchs
lift the blooming acacia into bright air.

Dreaming in Orange

1

Orioles disappear over a cloud wall.
Scraps of flame drift over the lake.

You grip your veil in the storm and pray
until your coral rosary beads
slide on strands of ochreous light,
away from you.

You and the fire haired girl you were
wait in the shadows to enter the garden running
to plunge your hands in dazzling water.

Your hands take on the color of rusty bricks.

2

He disappears around the corner
of your dreams for years

leaving his orange bicycle,
strands of his carroty hair,
scent of mango.

You let your own bicycle touch
the wall his body brushed against.
For a minute all the windows in the bricks
are his eyes.

Imagine you hear him
say *egrets* as a verb
meaning to vanish in mist.

3

All at once persimmon letters
crowd on a soft cream page.
Verbs pause, with sound of *e*
in *mute* and *a* in *dream*,
whisper a language you don't recognize.

4

Walls of fire, wheels of cloud
orange the color of trumpet flowers.
So close to the weaving
you can't read the colors.

II

Solstice Suite: A poem sequence

What I seek: Simultaneity ~
the same light spreading everywhere.

~ Claude Monet

California Morning Song

Olive tree bent on the hill,
bathed in expectancy.
Lavender, and white stone.

Sea wind turns the world transparent.

Jade shell
Pink Perfection camellia
water-cuts in sand

mutate on the zigzag border
between wholeness and coming undone.

The horizon a gold line,
broken by tankers and tall ships,
between visible and unseen.

How loneliness ends
though you are far from home.

How a sailor becomes
the oceans she sails across.

Missing the Solstice

During the peppery dusk
the day a sotto voce conversation
between stone-washed sky and sun

between small tasks—
scrubbing floor, clawing weeds—
I search the warm drum of summer evening

the rising moon
a golden mask from the house of Atreus

and listen to an alien chant, heart
torn open to the world.

Look inside yourself.
Now, look deeper.

Galactic Music

If I could drift into the current,
to grow in the belly of the sea
or be taken to another shore

where the branches of oak trees
lean against a larger air—tips
scratching the moon

where a star, far from first light, hurtles
through space to my eyes.
Most nights I forget to look

or listen, rolling fits and starts,
the ululation beneath
rough surfaces.

All these years and I can't tell
what one bird says to another

what fish flashes silver
in the heron's beak, that strong bird's neck
still a question mark.

Transit of Venus

A chowder of clouds, so many
we could not see
Venus cross the sun
like a cat pushing
the orange ball aside
or how we get dizzy
in a stopped train
when the coach next door
pulls away.

A braid of California pelicans
claims the estuary
parting air and water in their dives.

In Minnesota
a procession of geese
through shifting grass.

In California I hear freeway
overlaid with sea.
The Minnesota overlay
is wind, the way
lace softens a wool blanket.

How all our transits lattice Earth.

Solstice Waters: Allegro

Mississippi River Solstice

Sun a wide open eye inside us,
we walk the old river bridge.
Water thunders over the dam,
shaking bridge and celebrants
who lean over the railings.

Solstice dancers above us wave
from roofs of converted mills.
In the park below they spin
scarlet streamers while horns and strings
pour concertos from green windows
sprouting beneath bushes and trees.

A man with a sign passes by
    Pagans turn to Jesus
while children on bicycles
swerve around him, laughing
at each other's jokes.

How Jesus of the light
would have loved this night
even as the day keels forward
coruscating across the great river.

We are all kneeling over the wild violet waters.
Even the riverboat captain bows as he travels
through the locks and praises the plunging,
the rising, everything alive and flowing.

Solstice Waters: Lento

Wedding Anniversary, Maligne Lake

Because river drills into heart of stone
the mountain rises

because cobalt predicts and anticipates
but water never waits

as we are with each other

wet limestone becomes travertine
becomes coliseum   calcite
feeds the yellow breasted warbler

as we are in each other

because melting turquoise mixes with ice
to sheer translucence—then rock grinds glacier
to create the blue of Lake Maligne
no sky that color   no blossom
an impressionist's hue

as we are made   for one landscape only

Scry

Maybe when there are no rules
in candle flame air,
only the rose of each lung blooming.

White spiral script on black stone,
what can I learn?

After days of rain, pond a lake
in wind, what comes next?

One frog chants, five ducklings drag
tiny green V's behind their mother.
The red fox lurks, hungry.

Night heron hunches toward her own face,
purple shawled, back each year
to the same branch.

This morning I watch the muskrat
swim his trail across water
dragging dolorous ribbons in his mouth.

His lidless eyes stare straight ahead—
ahead is all there is.

Serenade

At home in St. Paul voices plead
in alleyways of bells.
Tombs lean in rows and inside them
we laid our parents.

In the morning the boardwalk calls us.
Our grey Toyota on the freeway, a way to breathe
racing east, turning west. In all our farewells
we pray for the next day and the next.

I fly with you to Chiang Rai and Athens,
Scotland, roses, morning.
We watch dolphins like poems
from the shore among herons fishing.

Music lifts us, the aegis of orchestra,
insistent waves of cello, violin's blue mountains,
leaping voice of piano—the vibrato inside us,
the clarity of water on stone.

Over us, a cloud's bruised lid
with fisted cold, tears, light, owl swooping.
When the night is fire or river inside us,
and we have no lock to keep our love,

we have June light and music joining
the waters of your life, the waters of mine.

Solstice Canyon: Fantasy

Shadows in crevices
the shape of giant breasts and belly
egg shaped holes everywhere
doorways explaining the world.

Slanted light defines flesh
as golden island
fissure and future without need
of horizon.

On the mounds of Antelope Canyon
hand prints of wind,
spires emerge from the moon
revealed as midsummer river.

Dusk is a breathing field of horses
a quick bright tongue lick.

Every part   saying *yes*.

Song of Solstice Fire

Monet's last water lily paintings—
his pond without paths of light
without perspective

Blossoms swim into blues
stained glass in starlight

Green of seaweed rooted
writhing inside the wave

One clear crimson blossom
burns in the center

The light of the soul, a fire
moving the dark around.

III

Sometimes An Angel

. . . the source of prayer is not fear, but delight.

Marina Tsvetaeva ~ Earthly Traces

The Poet Goes Fishing

In memory of poet, Joyce Uhlir

When the tip of your rod
scribbles on air like a toddler's crayon

and the length of nervous fiberglass
bends to the pull of weed or pike

you struggle to your feet, most in love
with this questing.

When it first comes into view,
that mute silver flash

wends its way through
wavering fields of water.

Now when it could be fish
or angel

you stand, straining to hold
that almost cracking rod

like Abraham to his God, crying out,
Here I am

as the surface fractures, showering light.

Between Rivers

for Sylvie

Tell us, Orion, great hunter
while you pace our land,
where can we anchor the tents
of our many languages, our longings?
Who will hear us through the din
of so many singing tongues?

The moon crosses a black sky
thick with shrieks of hawk, crow, owl.
Words I've forgotten—
buried dialects, whole alphabets
on the far side of rivers

crowd my mouth adding weight
and grit to what can only sing,
a slow Irish rolling from my tongue
to my tiny, dark-haired granddaughter.

From her eyes, somewhere between
the depths of the Nile, the Rhine
and the verdant marshlands of the Shannon,
a question drifts through the reeds,
Where am I?

Here, child, is your home, your mother tongue.
To those who crossed borders, who entered
harbors to make it yours, *thank you.*
Orion will follow you, child, watching over
all the cities where you will live
all the landscapes you will love.

Palimpsest

If by truth you mean hands
shaping the vertebrae of stars

If by hands you mean oak branches
scratching the moon's face

If by branches you mean that sickle moon
lying on its side as if asking

If by moon you mean pillow, expectant
as we, fingers laced, walk dim streets

If by pillow you mean feather words
the breath of fasting lovers

If by words you mean answers
where the moon tilts on its side
like a burning blade

If by answer you mean bruised trees,
clouds, lights of a far-off city, or the way
your finger slides into my closed fist

trembling the lifeline, the way
your palms resurrect my breasts.

Coming Home

Both natives and visitors in this town
we linger at the windows of new restaurants
remembering barbers, tailors here in the fifties,
the way my father at ninety walked Cathedral hill
telling us stories of the stones.

St. Paul street names are weighty—
explorers, saints and robber barons.
That old man bent over the piano in the pub,
fingers blurring, brings back the revolving piano bar
at the top of the downtown Hilton
where we decided one night to get married
and celebrated by making pilgrimage,
kissing in front of churches, schools, playgrounds
that held our lives on hilltops and hollows of the city.

Starting at the marble block of illuminated cathedral,
we drove backward in time, down Summit Avenue
to the Victorian brownstone of the Christian Brothers
who had just released you back into the world
then farther west on Summit to Fairview
to the warm sandstone gold of convent on Randolph.
We honored thick doors I'd opened,
head and chest full of clouds.

North on Prior to Nativity, thickset church and school
on top of the hill. Inspired by groomed gardens,
we drove down Randolph to St. James,
humble river parish pressed to earth and shaped
like the bent back of laborers,
where the rag-tag mix of us—Irish, Italian, Hungarian
first generation Americans—learned to read.

Uphill again to our parents' small wood and stucco
houses, each rooted on either side of Snelling.
Our tires carved wedges of snow toward Minneapolis
where the Mississippi curves.
Churches connected the corners of our map
and each churchyard teemed with spirits,
generations of men and women who pushed behind us
shouting many-tongued blessings.

Down Grand at the old church transformed
into theater, we entered the packed nave.
In the sanctuary, a fiddler, a bassist,
a drummer played beneath stained glass
saints and music freed from the confines
of strings, reed, hide. *No Jesus, no Guadalupe—*
just strangers who couldn't stop smiling
and tapping their feet.

Days We Wear Like Earrings

A dangle of stone, earth's furniture
braids of tremble and shine
the swoon of life intending

nothing beyond
whatever plumps our silhouettes
a pagan banana

a shrine in a box
open wings of the blue morpho
green bolt of tourmaline.

Days that shimmer
in perfect balance like opals
asymmetrical settings

eternal as mountains
clouds of volcanic ash, cooled
a billion years ago

or the earringed man in Bangkok
riding an elephant along the four-lane
against traffic, just holding on.

The Dream Theater

We narrow into the house, the room, the bed,
where sleep begins its shunting.
You cradle your head
neat as note paper in an envelope of sheets,
while I act a princess who owns the stage.

The headboard is disturbed
by your uncomfortable skew, hands
like stubborn adverbs visiting your face,
your shoulder in a piquancy of dreams
where I can't intrude.

You are all I have gathered to me of otherness.
I am still learning to lock and unlock
our weathered libraries of love.

Now you face away from me in sleep.
An old woman doorkeeper, bread in her pocket,
turns the key that lets the night pass.

With your brain in italicized gloom,
your mouth a little open,
the dream comes on, a place to climb the dark.
A hundred minutes of illusion
flickers beneath our late stars.

Wounded Angel

Too many spires,
more bells than she had feathers.

Warm-hearted sins wearing crimson dresses
in blazing gardens waved her in.

She shed radiance, grace
a folded white robe at her breast.

Nude, alone as rain
many sleepless eyes on her body,
she thought of his desire.

Like the bleating wave tracing the line of foam,
she wanted to touch those fringes
of soul on his skin.

Everything moving up from trees ensured
earthiness of the heart,
a direct speaking from wounds.

Moon-like blades unlocked
the daily bread window.

She heard a roar of wings, her mind's body
ran through acres of time and wheat

until she fell, her bee hive flesh
sheltering one holy thing

a red-tipped feather from her unfinished
leave-taking wings.

Eve Remembers

For a while we were on fire,
all of it inspired by the body
on which the senses hung like fruit.

Didn't we pluck them
night after night, our moans
a guttural music
from another world?

I waited the hours for you.
You beckoned and I followed,
misunderstanding your desire,
leaving a trail of clothes
toward the bed.

Didn't we know
what we had chosen?
Desire over love.
Didn't we flare
like moon raked coals?

We rented a garden
to paint the arduous seasons.
Lived like hermit crabs in leased shells.
Earth quaked beneath our nakedness.

You made me the deceived
believer—one of those saints
who had the gift of dreaming.

Discarnate Woman

She clings to the forest road, listens to wind lick
maple, oak and pine, yearns for raspberries
brilliant in their ragged bush,
but leaves them for blackbirds and finches.

Never knew her own taste, only that he loved it.
Never knew her own sounds, only that he
made her growl, purr, a high-pitched keening note
bending from her soft animal body.

Now the wind-shaped birch is never
a young woman with wings, the old beech
just a beech, not sculpture, not torso,
not vagina once painted as woods by Klimt,
legs slammed into earth, wild with loss.

Between Time

Magnetic fields draw us to Light;
they move our limbs and thoughts.
~Rumi

I know this earth—long blades of grass
have probed me, proving full existence,
paint pots of clay, empty silos
ready to receive September wheat,
subdued harmonies of new mown hay,
clouds scarring the heavens with purple.

The sea is not my metaphor
though imprisoned spirits
of the rainbow which once clung
to water and light drift inside me.

These fields of shuck and stack.
Their umbratic borders fill me
with spring melt,
with visions, hanging epiphytes, prisms
like stones in the stomach of a swallow.

Rain returns to blown glass air and breath
is a numinous, ripe intrusion.

Lost: A Sister's Tale

Four black hawks circle the freeway at twilight
like the four lost brothers of a girl
walking across the fields

carrying her mother's ring tied to a handkerchief
a wooden stool, a loaf of bread
a pitcher of water to ease thirst.

So hard to keep an eye on her stumbling
through fallow fields, overgrown forests
even her brothers lose sight of her.

They beat their wings
cry their hoarse signal *kri–i, kri–i*

sister, sister in dark syllables
during their hunting hour

when rabbits and voles browse
the rustling grass and bits of violet cloud
break off to drift over eastern mountains.

They hover above and you
crane your neck as the sky
sucks you into blue

so high you forget where that girl was born,
in what century, country, village,
what your name was

the taste of your mother's bread, and this
longing that swallows all others.

The oldest brother breaks the circle
heading east and pulls the others, weaving
black and gold behind them.

Do they spot you, or some
crooked branch, twitching shadow?

Stygian wings streak the vineyard kingdom
of crows into blue hills and you wonder
if you'll reach the edge of the world

and enter the cavern
where hawk brothers sleep,

if you'll have time for a sip of wine
from each of four beakers, time to slip
your mother's ring into the last of them.

In which country has she left
her cumbersome stool, where is your cup?

When four hawks cleave the evening sky
and disappear, the air vibrates leave-taking.

Adapted from the Grimms' tale, "The Seven Ravens"

River Cop

The department didn't know what to do
with his large hands, deep anger,
so they gave him a boat, the river to patrol
uncharted territories, nude swimmers, drunken boaters.
He had rope swings to cut down every night.

They were startled by his zeal, the parade
of nude boys, each day's catch shivering in blankets
because he hid their clothes. Mother rode the bus
down to the station to claim my speechless brothers.

The Mississippi cut through sandstone cliffs,
wild bottoms of old St. Paul—the river cop's boat
a moving target as he chugged up and downriver
waving his gun, threatening to shoot stray dogs, swimmers,
hunters who daily slogged through mud and reeds
to check riverbank traps.

From the shelter of the river caves, boys stoned his boat,
but when they saw the river cop, who couldn't swim,
floundering in deep water, they rescued him.

One summer night, Bill and Jerry dragged
a small civil war cannon all the way to the caves
below Otto Street, where they loaded nuts and bolts.
Soon metal struck the river cop's boat, a hollow clang
echoing through the river chamber, shaking beer bottles
off the shelves of West Seventh Street bars.

Sirens filled the streets, but the police refused to chase
kids into caves where in the dark, under garlands of bats,
they toasted a new street legend.

Boys who would soon die in Vietnam
broke free of cramped yards,
never naming the violence that cut sweet and murky
as the Mississippi through their lives.

The Last Time

Bent like an iced birch in her wheelchair.
Sister Catherine waits for me to bring my father
to visit her at Villa Maria.

She collects the history of her river town,
Old Frontenac, but my father wants to talk
about their common history.

I listen to them, studying their language
and in my mind watch the dead
rubbing sand from their eyes in the light.

In Claddagh on Galway Bay they strayed
through terraced shells and gray-blue pebbles
searching for famine seaweed to eat.
Sea cliff full as a hive.

The O'Briens in Boston. The Lynches, all those priests.
The dead brothers, sister, mothers.
My mother, God rest her soul.

They crowd together on shoulders of rock
where the sun is warm, joints cracking.
Not entirely old, they begin to talk.

The sea licks pale lichen off the rocks
and everywhere the spirits are hungry.
They could last for weeks on crusts
left on your plate.

In the chapel my father pulls down the red
padded kneeler, and falls heavily onto it.
Catherine sits in her wheel chair in the aisle.
They make stations, recite decades,
sorrowful, glorious bead after well-thumbed bead.

Without them, I would be a stranger.
I study the twilit crimson and cobalt
of the perfect rose window above the altar.
Soon they will both be gone.

Both Ways

In dingy schools, cramped rooms,
elms beating at the windows,
rain dictating its own orthography,
they gripped crumbling chalk
in fingers black with ink.
They fed wide-open minds
to calm our hungry turbulence.

In my chaotic girlhood I followed
these outmoded women in black,
so much like myself
and completely other.

What was it, the mystery
beneath black serge, nylon veil,
linen wimple, gimp over the breast?
Only face and hands available
to my curious eyes.

Now when I stand in front of my class,
the nuns gaze at me from the back of the room,
shake their heads, disapprove,
correct my mistakes
with the truculence of the dead.

Sometimes only their names
wind paths in the wood of the pews—
Margaret, Clare, Mary Honor, Victoria.

I hear the voice of their exhaustion,
see the emptiness which hid
the shining core of their lives.

In my mind nuns nod and smile
on their way to the convent,
still climb wooden steps
to tiny rooms or kneel in chapel.

Sometimes God plays Bach
inside their bones
or rises
into the ear of the wind
like a flaming hill of poppies.

Bridge

Swept along in traffic on 35E, no time at all
to honor this place, my old neighborhood in ruins.

In one second, wheels cross my brothers' bedroom
with the nursery rhyme floor and the closet where
G.I. Joe and their baseballs were stored.

Another second and I'm breathing coal smoke
back on the street where it poured from chimneys
over icy rooftops on winter mornings.

Steaming cream of wheat with milk fresh off the porch
before it froze. Then find a warm vent to dress by,
slacks under my skirt, scarf over my nose
for the trudge down West Seventh to school.
Frost lined my lashes, wind bent my neck.

I miss all the landmarks—Mr. Thin's outhouse, empty lot,
florist shop once standing where I'm driving now.

The house went first, then the elm trees.
It's not that I remember halcyon days,
chaos of boys shouting, fights I ran from
to Kathy Brown's—the one place still standing.

I still love, as my brothers do, those narrow streets,
windows lit up at night. One summer,
kids from West Seventh nearly blew up the pilings
on the Mississippi river bridge
through the wild heart of old Crosby Farm.
I was gone by then, but I know who did it.

Sometimes An Angel

Rain pounds through the palm fronds.
We are all looking for an ark.
Once I knelt, begged to be holy,
then I walked away. In the rain, a stranger
resembles my seventh grade teacher,
small intense grey-haired nun
who refused to talk to me.

Have you forgiven me for leaving you,
for writing my resistance?
In dreams I enter a church built like a ship
where she waits at the altar,
her face lit as if she were one of the angels,
all fire, opening the tight knot at the breast.

Rain pounds earth, ancient repeating rhythms.
We are all in need of forgiveness.
There was a time when I was free
and a time when I opened my hands.
It was summer, riding through the Appalachians
toward Cumberland Gap with my husband.

I held myself off the backseat
as we bounced over ruts,
afraid for the child, the passenger in my womb.
That narrow potholed road, oak and pine
draped with kudzu on both sides,
a border dividing my life.

I held a clay bowl offering love,
reclaiming it whenever I wanted,
a wild good plumbing deep.
Love always there for taking
and I in its thrall.

IV

Poppies In The Ruins

The way we are living,
timorous or bold,
will have been our life.

Seamus Heaney ~ Elegy

The Road

Time thick in your throat on the road to the land of the dead.
~*Theo Dorgan*

Way before Giza where she lay
in a sarcophagus, the pharaohs
being compact creatures like herself.

Before she left the chant and trembling
in Malta's Hypogeum,
womb deep inside the earth.

Long before Glastonbury,
she signaled boats from the Tor.
Before Malin Head, another ship's graveyard
crashed around her.
Before there was a lighthouse
on Inish Trahull, earth's oldest naked stone.

Even before she lived in the abbey in Paris,
her eyes filled with the wraiths
of women who came to wooden gates
carrying sick bodies of their children.

Way before the windowless house
on the Mississippi, or the convent walls
she knew were unnatural for a girl with wings.

She took a wrong turn somewhere,
but that was before she followed
cracks in stone where the light inside
breaks through into meadowsweet and gorse,
all thorns, no leaves, golden blooms.

Poppies In The Ruins

Heart strong as split stone,
I stumble on the path
between life and death,

remembering the mountain of Ephesus
where shards of marble survive
violent sunlight.
The wind in bright heat
hisses like winter in crevices of stone.

Scarlet poppies fill the cracks
where two walls of rubble meet
and the dry creek bed tumbles away
what's left of present and past.

When the bus dropped the two of us
on a corner in a small Turkish town,
I knew it was an ending and beginning.
Lost in drenching rain, crumble, vespa roar
it was possible to laugh, to find abundance.

The prayer call from loud speakers
on tiled roofs shattered the air.

Marriage Song

for Ann and Andrew

Who stands here? Our children
the tower of stories we built through long dark
crow winters, summers woven with light.

Once the day began with laughter and cheerios,
parents watching Andrew run,
parents watching Ann dance—

then both of our children gone
together, the way trees endure the wind,
thin-skinned birch, or rough oak,

giving all they are without resistance.
As clouds contest clouds
and wind makes a sea noise

love will unstitch them,
burn them like berries in juniper,
sing them one eternal note.

Epithalamion for Miranda and Timothy

Old names, old souls
you brought noise to our lives,
made us *mother, father.*

You brought us words
pouring from small mouths,
new worlds exploding
from child-seats in cars, on bicycles,
under our feet, just-born sentences
trailing us around the house.

Push the needle, toddler Miranda
always said, *Push the needle,*
when she wanted people to get to the point.
She was already there.

When I say timber nothing falls,
Tim announced at two
as he pushed open another door.

Timothy Miranda
may you go farther and deeper
into the wild, evanescent
life of this planet.

May everything you love
teach you how to live.
May you make stories, new from old.
May everything you grieve
teach you music.

May you follow the flute
and rattle of your dreams.

Painting the Walls

Life is a fall down a well
~A Buddhist monk

My mother's fingers never stopped twisting
for sons in Korea, Vietnam, somewhere in the streets.
You and I prayed, sang in stadiums, not churches,
each night counting the dead.

Through that violent winter, we argued
over draft-cards, afraid of prison, not knowing
how to find our voices, how to love
in a world that war was ending.

Now, children gone West and East, we are alone
again and still young ones die—here in distant lands—
our past, our present.
Helpless, helpless, helpless, helpless. . .
Neil Young's voice, a crackle of notes
from the stereo, another kind of burning.

History forgets to remember
the stumbling walk of the sun across water,
wind that keeps grieving around the corners
of the black monument.

Forget your angry voice, my exhausted dreams,
how time is life in reverse.
What can we do but leave messages on walls
for those who might remember?
What can we do but hold hands as we fall
down the well of the time we are making?

Cathedral Grove—Muir Woods

These redwoods hiss news
we've never noticed before.

Maps for a wanderer, they
wrap us in rough shadow.

Familial circles bear one another,
share water, wood, fog and needle.

Bear throat
egress of growl.
Deer-blink avenue
where spider drops her sac.

Vertical horizons, ravine of leaves.
Bark caverns
scarified calligraphies.

Leaf ears in the forest
catch little flies.

Green cuppings, like begging bowls
at invisible crossroads
take each offering
even the one that kills.

Missing the Monarch

Her flutter of black-on-gold always
led you through musk roses and clover,
you, reflecting on the difference
between hope and faith, but in the end
steering your own uncertain path.

Now cardinal, oriole, jay
steeped in tender sunrise
promise more than the day ahead—
all its milky hours undiscovered.

They raise expectations
for the absent—filigreed orange
wings hovering at first light
over fields of milkweed.

Is it ignorance that leads you
to side with optimists who blithely
predict the flaming one
will return some other year
warmer or wetter than this one?

Monarch always commanded you
not to let your thoughts drift
but to follow her as she ascended
into dizzy brightening air.
What was her meaning?
All, everything. . .

Invitation

Close to the edge of the sea where I walk
tides, cliffs, flight paths,
gulls and pelicans exult and dive
then bank on invisible airways.

Sweet William, wild mustard,
wedding colors gable the path.
I inhale their scent of coconut,
smell sunlight, the way a child does.

Suddenly a white field opens
to sea birling around rocks,
scraps of music, voices calling.

Later, fretting in traffic,
I try to remember
melodies, flocks of finches
pulsing in my ear.

Too late to know which spirits
sang, and if I'm the one
they wanted.

Beach Roses, Sea Grass

Swagged in mist, lavender froth of waves
in wind, young egrets fishing,
the path curves along the shore.
At the stone railroad bridge you cross
the river, walking the tunnel of track
until you clear bamboo forest,
see the river of lights on the 101,
turn west to pelicans, palms, sunset
breaking on water and stone.

Time and sand thick in your throat,
you come upon the half buried gun turret.
Its ghosts slipped away long ago,
canteens and helmets turned to rust,
nameless soldiers of the forties who breathed
your childhood air.

Cracked concrete memories of war and fear
turn you back the way you came
across the bridge, the narrow path along the beach
away from the land of the quiet dead
to the peopled boardwalk, apartment door
lit lamp, Mozart, notebook, husband.

You breathe knowing you are blest.
On the dark beach the gun turret,
obliterated by sea foam during high tide,
draped in sea weed during low,
is an ear listening for the rising moon.
Time to be what you will be.

If Not Snow

Why fight it? Hundreds
of work bound souls stacked up,

the river deepening toward its mouth.
Grey sky, city, hissing grey roads.

Let's say you long to break out.
You need to feel surf pound,

burn you clean, body opening to heat.
Instead you are caught in rush hour

where billboards shoulder each other
above freeway barriers and car dealer signs,

gas stations, each with locked-in attendant.
Half here, half nowhere, you're beginning

to wonder what the soul can fasten to.
The vast flotilla of flakes

adrift across the mind of the sky. White birds
gather above us, cover our world

with their own blank-eyed, implacable ending.

Without Blessing

I don't remember my mother's arms.
Softly rocked, I must have nested
in the velvet of her lap, rosy-cheeked,
waking, head turning to sound.

But I had a stubborn streak.
I wanted to fashion myself
from my own rib.

I remember my arms
pulling the door open,
the transparent curtains
harboring the glow of her fingers,
the breath half taken
waiting on her face.

Unloosened from her arms
I flew away, heady with daring,
desperate to not be her,
flying into the sea coil of a song,
the contours of a life shaped
more by chance than choice.

What's left, now that she is gone?
A bright-eyed inquisition
in her mirrored gaze.

Snow

The day my mother died
snow settled on slick streets
in the kingdom of crows.

Yellow grass under bulbs of ice,
seeds gathered in dark eddies
waited for the surge of impatient water
to move them along.

Then the drifts began to melt.
Feathery flakes,
the one who birthed me
vanished.

My hands in snow water
ice cold earth
running between my fingers.

There is nothing to hold onto
and nothing holds onto us.

At the end my mother knew
everything that had been given
would be carried away.

Aging in Ephesus

In a tea garden in the small Turkish town
four small tables with chairs.
Trees muffle the clamor of motorbikes.
Tall stones surround a decaying bathhouse,
all orange in slanting light.

An innkeeper smiling below a moustache bows,
pours wine and tea served with small silver spoons.
All time gathered in this quiet,
grey and white kittens winding around my legs.
In the field a column from the temple of Artemis.
On the hill above, ruins and the tomb of St. John.

Storks, gulls, soft conversation,
even as the call for prayer resounds
from low roofs of white washed houses.
A kingdom of stone paths,
wild hollyhocks and kittens' mewling.
After sunset, a whole fish, grilled, dressed
with tomatoes and cumin, appears on a plate.
I want to kiss it.

A Walk in the Cotswold

I carry my grief to night's crying gate
to catch the sun's last shining.

Tramp across the fields, spring sunset,
a meadowlark, muddy road winding down
to the church, a tree-lined cloister.

Through the graveyard, centuries thrown together
on leaning stones, teeth in earth's wet mouth,
yew trees and mistletoe in berry.

Between the thatched roofed houses,
sloping cobblestones, gardens of daffodils,
iris, pansies rustling with sparrows.

An old man and woman close their red door,
stop at other gates, stroll to the low-roofed pub,
stone fireplace sided with baking ledges,
cups and steins on hooks.

A grey cat crouches at the window staring
at bodies huddled over pints and shepherd's pie.

Calling the world changeless
changes everything.

The sun pours light toward my love
on the other side of the world.

Everything's changed except the heart.

Field Walking in County Donegal

I stumbled upon a fairy fort
a sacred circle of large stones.
The wind a sea surge
in a holly tree,
peacock-tail crown
turned from a bramble
hedge to an emerald and amber
soon to be flaming bowl
of mysteries and whispers.

Sky a frosted pane, a tumble of crows.
Fox-red bracken feathered
chocolate rabbit holes.

I turned around inside the circle
three times, sun-wise
as my grandmother said.

Nothing happened.
I climbed high, stony Marmore Pass,
stopped at the shrine of St. Columba
its paper prayers flapping in wind,
passed wilted flowers in jars
to the holy well, glint of dropped coins.

Down I gazed on the field
the stones, the fairy tree, the sea
rapt in salty concentration,
and I wondered if the world
could ever be changed
by my shambling, ancient, field-love.

Burnt Dress

Even in old age I need you,
your voice a ululation
across a meadow tracked
by the capricious ash-grey hare.

Your words sprout
from my heart like mallow.
You tell me to claim
the wildness I once wanted.
Your words, stones
I keep fingering.

Beauty walks this world aging everything—
each colonnade, leaf, sparrow,
lintel, scarf, water bird.

I am an angel in a burnt dress.

I call you now from the square,
stalls hung with yellow roses and handbags.
So much stone here,
a star-fall of stained glass.

One egret in a field,
the loneliness
of angels without
even the body of a shadow.

My breath spread so thin
that nothing's left but bone
white emptiness, whisper of ruins.

Weaving, forever weaving
into and out of this world.

Wheatfield

Our bodies were the color of wheat,
a field near the Mississippi
where long necked geese
spread their wings over marshes, wings
carrying them on spirals of wind.

We skimmed across the world, holding
each other, skin sweet with grass scent,
warm with sun that still floods our mornings.
Below us green banks tangled,
violets and cowslips, purple spikes
of lupine, fingers of wild asparagus.

Every day we are older
with each new thing we ignore,
how falling oak leaves blanket
beds of moss, oak leaf percussion
nothing like beech or pine,
the way each green makes love
to its shadow.

The way your body marries the slope of mine.
All these things clear now
as when we first lay flank to flank
and let ourselves be borne to the river marshes
where wheat ripples in the sun.

It's not the bird but the branch that sings
caprice on the wind where geese
tilt their long gray necks like rudders,
lift into one blue V,
calling as they spin out above us.
Sex, color and music gathering darkness.

Angels

Blue between their bones
gathering to a star in our violet throats,
glass voices stain the air, a flock
of nightingales abandoned in winter.

Who prolong the growing fields
lift away darkness, half miracles
in the night, like stars that won't behave,
twisting on a rope of flowers.

Whose wings carry starlings
through meadows unherbed
by a thousand careless feet

Through hurricanes of violence
splintering cities, setting them down
unharmed in a wheat field.

Rivers pouring blindly, nameless roads
curving through the breast,
atoms splitting atoms

Through villages of mysteries,
caverns of the ocean gods, eight-armed
cupids, seashell weddings.

Poets of the afterlife
beating new rhythms for dusk and dawn
murmuring rhymes until the timekeeper
angel arrives in her burning boat.

Created after our own form—
earth-colored clear-breasted angels
like barely moving water
over a snowfield

Giving everything to return us
to the bright endangered earth.

The Eyes of the Saints

Keep custody of your eyes, the nuns told us.
If your eye is holy, your whole body
will fill with light.

We walked the cloister, eyes down,
through reflection and shadow
sending hand signals, mudras:
How heavy is your heart today?
Can we talk later?
Meet me in the laundry room or attic.

Our gaze locked on the ground,
fears heavy inside us,
what was there to keep, what to lose?

These days my eyes know
the weight of lightless hours
when shadows beside my bed are solid
and I am shadow to what has not yet happened.

All these years avoiding—
that bear in the deep woods,
waves rolling over the bow of the boat.

Yet it still approaches—what will destroy me,
hidden beneath the woven net of daily
air and apples, the sidewalk crack.

Jesus said the eye is a lamp,
a burning incandescence,
an oil I must pour more generously
over the waves of darkness.

What's that ripping sound?
Just my unholy eyes
learning to open the dark,
to discern each petal of the wood lily,
delicate wings of the damsel fly.

NOTES

Because of the long term poetry exchange between the California poet, Maia, and myself, several of the poems in this manuscript were inspired by her work. I acknowledge this debt of creative inspiration. The following six poems in particular are indebted to her work. Analemma—inspired by *Absence* and *Lost*, italicized line from *Lost*; Burnt Dress—inspired by *White Amaryllis* and *Great Blue Heron*; Coming Home—italicized lines adapted from *Strangers*; Dreaming In Orange—owes a debt to *Eight Dreams of Forgetting*; The Vastness Around Her—italicized lines are from *Persephone By The Sea*; Snow—inspired by *Blue Grouse*.

Tapestries
The five "Lady and the Unicorn" tapestries hang in Musée de Cluny, Musée National du Moyan Age in Paris. *A mon seul désir* is the name of one of them.
The italicized lines are quoted from "Unicorn" in my previous book, *The Illuminations*.
The Bayeaux Tapestry was created in 1066 by Matilda, wife of William the Conqueror, to mark the Norman conquest of England. It hangs in Bayeaux, France.

Gardens of Paris
Rodin's sculpture "The Thinker" can be found in the gardens of the Rodin Museum in Paris. The thirteenth century stained glass windows of La Sainte-Chapelle are known for jewel tones of red and blue.

One Hundred Sand and Flower Carpets
Many people of Guatemala create these incredible works of transitory art for Lenten processions.

Ordinary Time is the title of a poetry book by Marie Howe.

Shifting Time
This poem owes a debt to poems by Adam Zagajewski in *Eternal Enemies.*

The Dream Theater owes a debt to Medbh McGuckian
The title *Blind, Dazzled, Winged* is adapted from the title of a McGuckian poem.

Beach Roses, Sea Grass was inspired by Theo Dorgan's *Wild Orchids, Windflowers.*

Field Walking in County Donegal
Marmore Mountain is in the Inishowen Penninsula, County Donegal, Ireland.

ABOUT THE COVER ARTIST

Hervé Constant is a London-based French artist. He was born in Casablanca, Morocco. He studied theatre acting at the Conservatoire de Toulon before obtaining a grant to further his studies at the Ecole Nationale Superieure des Arts et Techniques du Theatre in Paris. Hervé's work is a mixture of different interests, social and cultural influences. His work is internationally exhibited and collected. Recent projects involve video, photos and sounds and Artist's Books. **www.herveconstant.co.uk**

ABOUT THE AUTHOR

Mary Kay Rummel is honored to be the first Poet Laureate of Ventura County, CA. *The Lifeline Trembles*, a co-winner of the 2014 Blue Light Press Award is her seventh book of poetry. Blue Light Press published her previous book, *What's Left is the Singing*, in 2010. Her work has appeared in numerous regional and national literary journals and anthologies and has received many awards, including four Pushcart nominations. Mary Kay has read in many venues in the US and London, and has been a featured reader at poetry festivals including Ojai and San Luis Obisbo, CA. She often performs poetry with musicians. A professor emerita from the University of Minnesota, Duluth, she and her husband, Conrad, teach part time at California State University, Channel Islands. They live and play with their grand children in California and Minnesota. See **marykayrummel. com** and Poet Laureate Ventura County (on facebook).

Other Poetry Books by Mary Kay Rummel

What's Left Is The Singing (Blue Light Press, 2010)
Love in the End: A chapbook (Bright Hill Press, 2008);
The Illuminations (Cherry Grove, 2006);
Green Journey, Red Bird (Loonfeather Press, 2000);
The Long Journey Into North: A chapbook (1999) Juniper Press;
This Body She's Entered, (1989) A Minnesota Voices Award Winner
at New Rivers Press, Finalist for a Minnesota Book Award.

Recent anthologies containing her work include:

The Wind Blows, The Ice Breaks (Nodin Press); *A Bird Black As The Sun*
(Green Poet Press); *Meditations on Divine Names* (Moonrise Press);
Daring to Repair (Wising Up Press); *The Heart of All That is: Reflections
on Home* (Holy Cow! Press); *St. Paul Almanac* (Arcata Press); *Nimrod*
(University of Tulsa); *ASKEW*; *First Water: Best of Pirene's Fountain*
(Glass Lyre Press); *Woman in Metaphor: An anthology of poems inspired
by the paintings of Stephen Linsteadt* (Natural Healing House Press);
River of Earth and Sky: Poems for the 21st Century (Blue Light Press).

Printed in The United States of America

www.ingramcontent.com/pod-product-compliance
Lightning Source LLC
Chambersburg PA
CBHW022034090426
42741CB00007B/1059